CONTENTS

Published 2019.
Little Brother Books, Ground Floor,
23 Southernhay East, Exeter, Devon, EX1 1QL

Printed in Poland.

books@littlebrotherbooks.co.uk |
www.littlebrotherbooks.co.uk

The Little Brother Books trademark, email
and website addresses and the Pop Winners
logo and imprint are sole and exclusive
properties of Little Brother Books Limited.

Images used under license from PA Images
and Shutterstock.com.

PERRIE

The bubbly, boho one!

NAME: Perrie Edwards
BIRTHDAY: 10th July, 1993
STAR SIGN: Cancer
HOME TOWN: South Shields

Nicknames

Perrie Louise Edwards, to give her her full name, is also known as **PERIWINKLE** or **PEZ**. Her Dad likes to call her **PEP**. That's a lot of Ps!

Little Mix LOLs

Perrie reckons the girls have such a laugh together that every day is like a stand-up comedy sketch! She loves the hilare Little Mix world which makes her cry with laughter.

GOING LIVE

Perrie's fave memory of performing live is at the X Factor final in Wembley Arena. In front of an audience of 10,000 (not to mention the 10 million watching at home!) Little Mix totally smashed it and made history by becoming the first group to win the show. Perrie describes the experience as 'insane', but in a good way, of course!

Socials

@littlemix   @LittleMix

JESY

The confident, rocky one!

NAME: Jesy Nelson
BIRTHDAY: 14th June, 1991
STAR SIGN: Gemini
HOME TOWN: Romford

EARLY DAYS

Jesy went to stage school as a child so has been in the limelight from an early age. Singing and performing have always been her jam.

DON'T CARE

Strong Woman

Jesy has learnt not to care about what other people say about her and to be happy with who she is. This positive attitude spills out into everything she does and has made her the strong, confident woman she is today. What an inspo!

Big Girls Do Cry!

Down-to-earth Jesy is totally in touch with her feelings and isn't afraid to let them show. So many things bring a tear to her eye, including her fam being upset and if the other Little Mixers have been hurt. She also cries bucket-loads with laughter too!

Socials

📷 @littlemix   🐦 @LittleMix

LEIGH-ANNE

The caring, fashionable one!

NAME: Leigh-Anne Pinnock
BIRTHDAY: 4th October, 1991
STAR SIGN: Libra
HOME TOWN: High Wycombe

INSPO IDOLS

American diva Mariah Carey first inspired Leigh-Anne to sing and it's fearless Rihanna who is her confidence inspo. But when it comes to music, her biggest inspiration of all is the king of pop himself, Michael Jackson.

Leigh-Anne's got Bieber fever!

Special Moment

There have been a million amazing LM moments but one that stands out for Leigh-Anne is selling out the O2 on the group's first arena tour. Standing in front of the thousands of fans who were there just to see the girls made Leigh-Anne burst into tears. But don't worry, they were tears of happiness, she just couldn't believe her dream had finally come true!

Starstruck!

Even though she's a super famous member of the biggest girl group in the world, Leigh-Anne is still in awe of other celebs. Once, when Justin Bieber popped into Little Mix's dressing room to say hi at an awards show, poor Leigh-Anne was so starstruck she couldn't speak!

Socials

 @littlemix  @LittleMix

JADE

The cute, chilled one!

NAME: Jade Thirlwall
BIRTHDAY: 26th December, 1992
STAR SIGN: Capricorn
HOME TOWN: South Shields

AKA

At school Jade was known as Pickle because she was so small you could fit her into a jar! The other Little Mixers call her Jadey or Poopey – charming!

Yep!

Pop Idol

Please note, this is a photo of Diana Ross NOT Jade's mam!

You can thank Diana Ross for getting Jade into singing. As a young girl, Jade idolised her, watching all of her videos and copying everything she did. The wannabe singer was convinced that her own mum was actually Diana Ross – when she went to play bingo with her friends, Jade thought she was off to another concert! How adorbs is that!

BANTS AND LOLS

Jade reckons the girls' funniest moments happen when they're tired and delirious and the banter just flows. So feel sorry for anyone who has to interview them after an all-nighter!

Socials

 @littlemix   @LittleMix

PICTURE PUZZLES

There's a whole load of Little Mix fun packed onto these pages for you to enjoy!

#SelfieFail

Which Little Mixer has taken this blurred selfie?

Perrie

Spot It

Which of these Leigh-Anne pix is the odd one out?

A   B   C

la-la ♥ music

Jade in the Shade!

Which of these shadows matches this picture of Jade exactly?

A   B   C

OOPS!

Award Dash

LM have won another award – hurray! But Jesy's misplaced it – boo! Which trail will lead her to the missing trophy?

A   B   C

LM HIGHLIGHTS

It's been a busy time in Little Mix Land recently – here's some of what the girls have been up to and a taste of things to come...

Get the lowdown on the highlights!

Bring on the Brit!

Little Mix were super excited to bag their second Brit at the 2019 Brit Awards. The girls scooped the British Artist Video of the Year award for *Woman Like Me*.

The hilare video shows the Mixers failing epically at traditional female roles but being completely unfazed by it. Set in an English stately home, the whole thing screams 'girls are awesome' (just in case you didn't already know!).

The Mixers also performed live at the awards ceremony. Popping in pink, the girls treated viewers to a high energy performance of *Woman Like Me*.

YES

Little Mix - Woman Like Me (Official Video) ft. Nicki Minaj

LM5 Tour

The Mixers are kicking off their 6th tour, LM5, in Spain. After performing to fans across Europe, they'll hit various venues in the UK and Ireland in October and November before heading down under to perform in Australia. It promises to be a show-stopping, hit-blasting, outfit-changing extravaganza! But TBH you wouldn't expect anything less from these four superstars!

Going Global

The girls picked up a double whammy at the Global Awards 2019, nabbing Best Group and Best Song for *Woman Like Me*. Best Group was voted for by the public so Little Mix have their army of fans to thank for that one!

Did you vote for Little Mix?

Yes ☐   No ☑

Be the Light

JESY'S STORY

Jesy is working on a documentary with the BBC looking at body image and mental health. Having suffered from mental health problems herself, Jesy hopes she'll be able to make a difference to the lives of others through this important project. As well as telling her own story, Jesy will be looking at how social media is effecting young people's health. Follow Jesy on Instagram for more updates. @JesyNelson

When does this multi-tasking popstar/designer/ business woman find time to sleep?!

Beach Ready!

As well as being a quarter of the biggest gal group in the world, Leigh-Anne has somehow found time to launch her own range of swimwear! In 'A' Seashell makes bikinis for all body shapes and Leigh-Anne hopes that anyone can wear and feel good in her fierce designs.

proud of me

What's your beachwear style?
Bold bikini ☐
Cute one-piece ☑
Shorts and tee combo ☐

13

Festival Fun

Little Mix rocked the main stage at Radio 1's Big Weekend 2019. Tickets to the event in Middlesbrough were quickly snapped up and the girls joined the likes of Miley Cyrus, James Arthur and Rita Ora at the star-studded fest.

ROCK

Cool

Aiming High

Adventurous Jade and Leigh-Anne climbed Mount Kilimanjaro, the biggest mountain in Africa, to raise money for Comic Relief. The girls joined a team of celebs for the week-long trek to the summit. They may have faced altitude sickness, exhaustion and blisters along the way, but the Mixers were still smiling when they reached the top.

#TheseGirlsCan

Which emoji would you award Jade and Leigh-Anne for their awesome achievement?

Over to you!

Have your say on Little Mix's highlights.

MY FAVOURITE LITTLE MIX HIGHLIGHT IS

_____

_____

_____

THE EVENT I WISH I'D BEEN AT IS

_____

_____

_____

MY AWARD FOR BIGGEST INSPO GOES TO

FOR
_____

FOR
_____

FOR
_____

TOP 10 TWEETS

There are squillions of inspiring, amusing and feel-good @LittleMix tweets. Here's a countdown of 10 of the best.

ADORBS!

10 Leigh-Anne was super-excited about the launch of her new swimwear range.

> **Little Mix** ✔
> @LittleMix   Follow ⌄
>
> Guys @inaseashell is officially OUT NOW thank you for your support! I love you guys so much! Can't wait to see you rocking it! inaseashell.co.uk x Leigh

AWWWWWW!

9 The girls got all nostalgic with this cute tweet about friendship.

> **Little Mix** ✔
> @LittleMix   Follow ⌄
>
> Unbelievable. The #HairMusicVideo came out exactly three years ago today!
> This video is all about friendship, which pretty much sums us up 🖤
> The girls x

7 Little Mix shared this exciting tweet which rates them at number one for most streamed girl group of all time on Spotify.

> **Little Mix Updates**   Follow ⌄
> @ShadyMixerFacts
>
> The Top 5 Most Streamed Girl Groups of All Time on Spotify:

#	ARTIST	TOTAL STREAMS
1	Little Mix	3,356,564,488
2	Fifth Harmony	3,347,144,021
3	Destiny's Child	1,249,541,808
4	BLACKPINK	1,021,089,585
5	The Pussycat Dolls	718,888,794

> 7:00 AM - 24 Mar 2019
>
> 1,157 Retweets 4,935 Likes
>
> 💬 56   🔁 1.2K   ♡ 4.9K

8 Leigh-Anne posted this heartfelt message after doing an interview with Glamour mag where she spoke about dealing with online racism.

> **Little Mix** ✔
> @LittleMix   Follow ⌄
>
> Thank you for giving me the opportunity to speak up on something so close to my heart! It means so much 🖤🖤🖤 Leigh

RESULT!

6 Rays of Sunshine is a charity that grants wishes to seriously ill children. The girls posted this lovely message after going to its Wish Day event.

Little Mix ✓
@LittleMix

Follow ⌄

We LOVED meeting these brave and inspiring children at our @RaysofSunshine wish day! We're honoured to be ambassadors for this amazing charity, thanks for having us 🖤 the girls x

5 Riding on a high after winning at the 2019 Brit Awards, Little Mix couldn't wait to thank their fans.

Little Mix ✓
@LittleMix

Follow ⌄

We just can't thank you enough. We bang on about how amazing you are but we really do have the best fans in the world!
We really did just go and win Best British Video 🖤🖤🖤🖤🖤🖤
So grateful we get to do what we love with each other and celebrate in ways like this!
the girls x

4 After Perrie bravely spoke out to her Instagram followers about suffering from panic attacks, Capital FM posted this message of support.

Capital ✓
@CapitalOfficial

Follow ⌄

Perrie Edwards has bravely opened up about her anxiety battle and she's our hero 🖤 @LittleMix

62 👤

3 Custodian of Knebworth House, Henry Cobbold, posted this hilare tweet after the Mixers filmed their *Woman Like Me* video at the stately home.

Henry Cobbold
@HenryCobboldKH

Follow

Thanks to @LittleMix for popping by to do the ironing, some hoovering and some flower arranging at #KnebworthHouse - you've got the job. When can you start?
youtu.be/fSOpiZo1BAA #LittleMix @KnebworthHouse

2 On International Women's Day @LittleMix gave a shout out to all those strong women who came before them. #GirlsAreAwesome

Little Mix ✓
@LittleMix

Follow ⌄

Thank you to all the women who paved the way for us, we couldn't have got here without you 🖤 Happy International Women's Day 🖤 #IWD2019
the girls x

17 🖤

1 @LittleMix retweeted this exciting news about Jade featuring in the Urban Dictionary. Well done, pet!

Tilz
@wheeler_mixer

Follow

Ummm our girls are an example in the urban dictionary #madeit wow I'm shook @LittleMix

10:49 pm   📶 68% 🔋

Telstra 📶

🔒 google.com.au   ↻

ⓘ   urbandictionary.com   ↔

URBAN DICTIONARY   Type any word...   ⤬

TOP DEFINITION

Nanite

Geordie slang for **goodnight**/nightnight most commonly used by Jade Thirlwall

Perrie: sleep well Jadey!
Jade: nanite Pez.

54 💬

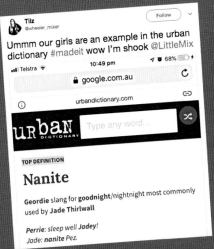

SUPERSIZE SEARCH

Can you find all of the LM inspired words hidden in this massive wordsearch?

```
D A F T D F A N S N H S Y I O A X B E Q
E A G J A S L F E N O R E B M U N D H R
X F N A C T S Q B T U E Y Z F A W S S Y
F A M C S W E J L I P T O B R R T Q O A
F G H S E R D B R I T A W A R D R X U O
J W E J K R F I H S O N D S A R F D T K
W G S I T R O C E L E F G U S A A D H R
M U B L A P S U Y X U M C Z C V N W S I
R T P J F S A B T T I Y L T W R S E H K
I Y S S J S D G H I A S O E R J L H I T
C O E I Y O E R T S N R T F R E U I E L
O D I S R N Y M J K L E P J D Q D I L R
N F T S O G H I A W Y C R U O T F S D N
S I I K S D F U I F V I D A S A L D S M
R T R E E Y D S N M A S Q K F G H J T R
D E B W O T T E B M O C Y W H G I H P Y
T H E R D E V S W X A S Q G H I L P F S
F N L Q J K D L S E R T R O M F O R D D
K S E W S D A I H Y K I T R E D F O P I
W D C E S A H K V L O F D H A M N D I S
```

- ☐ ALBUM
- ☐ CELEBRITIES
- ☐ SONG
- ☐ SOUTH SHIELDS
- ☐ BRIT AWARD
- ☐ TOUR
- ☐ X FACTOR
- ☐ FANS
- ☐ DANCE ROUTINE
- ☐ ROMFORD
- ☐ FAME
- ☐ VIDEO
- ☐ HIGH WYCOMBE
- ☐ NUMBER ONE
- ☑ ICONS

ANSWERS ON PAGES 76-77.

#BE YOUR SELFIE

Little Mix are taking selfies! Can you work out which member each pic is of?

Jade

Leigh-Anne

A

B

Jesy

Perrie

C

D

ANSWERS ON PAGES 76-77.

21

CHART-TOPPING CHOON!

Have a go at writing your own pop song using the Little Mix lyrics below. Add in some of your own words to make it personal to you.

The best songs are written from the heart!

Take a sip of my secret potion, I'll make you fall in love.

Get your killer heels, sneakers, pumps or lace up your boots.

Hey, how ya doing'? Sorry you can't get through.

Cause it don't matter who you are, you can be who you wanna be.

Oh, I need you more than words can say.

These wings are made to fly.

I was born without a zip on my mouth.

It's in his DNA and he just takes my breath away.

So it's hard not to fall when you feel like a cannonball.

Stay out all night, go where the music's loud.

All the girls on the block knockin' at my door.

MY LM PLAYLIST

My fave Little Mix song is

SHOUT OUT TO MY EX

Their best album IMO is

GLORY DAYS

The tune guaranteed to get me on the dance floor is

CANNONBALL

I'm all the way up, I swear you'll never, you'll never bring me down.

Write your hit song here.

GO!

23

WHO'S YOUR BESTIE?

Which one of LM would be your perf pal?
Answer the questions below to find out!

#BFFS

1

WHAT'S YOUR STYLE?

- 👍 A little bit edgy ☐
- 😐 Cute and coordinated ☐
- ♡ Cool but casual ☑
- 😄 Boho chic ☐

2

WHAT DO YOU HAVE MOST OF IN YOUR BEDROOM?

- 👍 Trainers ☐
- 😐 Books ☐
- ♡ Clothes ☐
- 😄 Teddies ☑

3

WHAT'S YOUR FAVE FOOD?

- 👍 Burger and chips ☐
- 😐 A homemade Sunday roast ☐
- ♡ Nachos with all the trimmings ☑
- 😄 A spicy curry ☐

4

HOW DO YOU LIKE TO CHILL?

- 👍 In front of the telly with a takeaway ☐
- 😐 With a pen and a puzzle book ☐
- ♡ Lounging in the sun ☐
- 😄 Spending time with the fam ☑

MOSTLY 👍 #2

Like Jesy, you're bold and brave and aren't afraid to tell it like it is. You two would definitely hit it off!

MOSTLY 😀

You're kind, thoughtful and calm just like Jade. You'd have the best time chillin' out together.

5

WHAT CAN'T YOU LIVE WITHOUT?

- 👍 Friends and family ✓
- 😀 Tea and biccies ☐
- ♥ My pets ☐
- 😆 My phone ☐

MOSTLY ♥ 2

You're fun to be around, confident and caring. Leigh-Anne would be lucky to have you as her BFF!

6

WHICH WORD BEST DESCRIBES YOU?

- 👍 Positive ✓
- 😀 Chilled ☐
- ♥ Confident ☐
- 😆 Funny ☐

MOSTLY 😂 2

You're fun to hang out with and are always up for a laff. You and Perrie would get on like a house on fire!

COOL COLLABS

How do you make Little Mix even more awesome? Team them up with other superstar singers, of course! Here are some of the Mix's best collaborations.

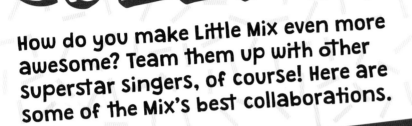

The Beginning

Way back in 2013, the girls were super excited to record their first collab with one of Jesy's musical icons, Missy Elliott. The American rapper featured on *How Ya Doin'?* from the *DNA* album.

Brit Nominee

LM teamed up with dancehall singer, rapper and DJ, Sean Paul, to record the catchy choon *Hair*. The song peaked at number 11 in the UK singles chart and was nominated for Best British Video of the Year at the 2016 Brit Awards. Not bad!

Super Stormzy

Stormzy rapped in Little Mix's 2016 hit *Power*. Taken from the *Glory Days* album, the high-energy, girl-power anthem peaked at number 6 proving that the girls are awesome (and Stormzy's not bad either!).

Shhhhhh, it's a Secret!

Global chart-topping singer, songwriter and dancer, Jason Derulo, joined the girls to record *Secret Love Song* in 2016. The pop ballad spent an impressive 25 weeks in the UK singles chart. That's a whole lotta love!

MY MUSIC

Girl Power!

The Mixers joined forces with rapping sensation, Nicki Minaj, to record their 2018 hit *Woman Like Me*. The powerful song, which won a Brit Award for its video, is all kinds of awesome!

Cool Combo

Remember when Little Mix teamed up with CNCO to remix CNCO's hit song *Reggaetón Lento*? With Spanish lyrics, a Latin American vibe and amaze vocals it's the ultimate girl band/boy band combo. In fact, you could say it's perfecto!

ROCK

Mix it Up

In July 2018, Little Mix released a remixed version of *Think About Us* featuring American rapper Ty Dolla $ign. The storming pop ballad had all the feels and stayed in the UK singles chart for 15 weeks.

SLOGAN TEES

Celebs love to let their t-shirts do the talking! Use the page opposite to design a super cool slogan tee for one of Little Mix.

This design is fierce!

#GUNIT #LEUK

YOU can be enything you WHATYOU to be what ever you what to !

Designed for _____Jesy_____ by _____Katie_____.

My tee is totally on fleek!

I'VE NAILED THE AESTHETIC!

#POSITIVEVIBES

Little Mix inspire their fans to be the people they want to be. Read more about their positive inspo below, then fill the fan file opposite.

Follow your Dreams

Little Mix are living examples of what can happen when you follow your dreams. They didn't give up and inspire their fans to do the same. "If you want something, work hard and you'll get it," Leigh-Anne advises in *Our World*, Little Mix's official biography.

Surround Yourself with Friends

●REC

The girls lead by example when it comes to being a fantastic friend. And their fans are their BFFs too! They always make time to interact with fans through Q&As on social media and by replying to posts. They'll never forget the driving force behind their fame.

Be Confident

Leigh-Anne says the best advice she's ever been given is, "to have confidence and believe I am the best" (*Our World*). Little's Mix's confidence shines through in everything they do and when you believe in yourself, anything is possible.

Love Yourself

Little Mix are loud and proud about loving themselves, flaws and all! The girls definitely own what makes them unique. In *Our World*, Perrie says, "Be yourself, never try to be something you're not." Wise words, Pez!

music

FAN FILE

I LOVE LITTLE MIX BECAUSE

....

....

MY FAVE MEMBER IS

ALL

THE BEST THINGS ABOUT HER ARE

THEY ARE ALL GREAT AT SINGING

LITTLE MIX HAVE INSPIRED ME TO

SING

THE ADVICE I WOULD
GIVE LITTLE MIX IS

....

....

**The positive words below can be
used to describe the Little Mixers.
Tick the ones that describe you too.**

Confident	☑	Talented	☑	Loyal	☑	Inspirational	☑
Kind	☑	Strong	☒	Hardworking	☑		
Brave	☑	Funny	☑	Thoughtful	☑	*pop*	

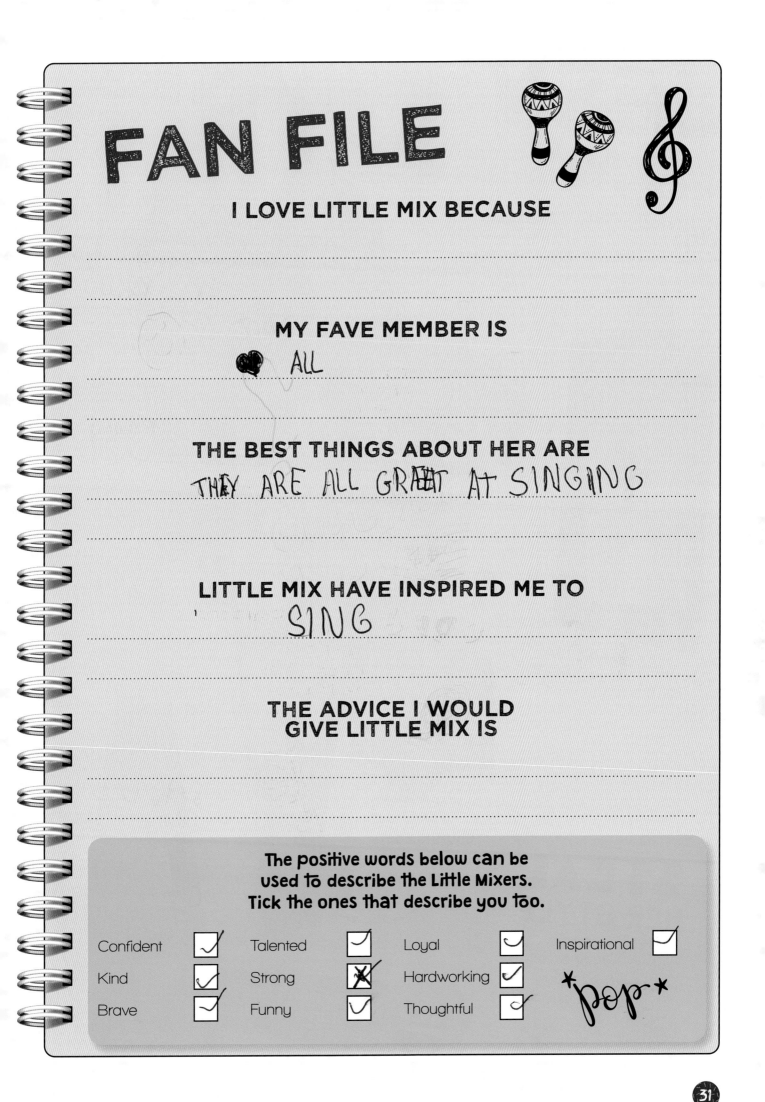

JESY

Cool, casual, rocky, feminine – Jesy's alternative wardrobe has it all!

Oversized coats are sooooo Jesy!

A celeb is never without her shades!

RAD

Jesy loves casual camo!

Jesy is red carpet ready in this rocky combo.

STEAL HER STYLE

Think camo prints, denim, lots of black, chunky footwear, fishnets and layers.

Chunky boots are practical and cool!

You won't lose her in a crowd!

JADE

Cute and preppy is Jade's signature style.

This baker boy hat is totally Jade.

A cheeky flash of midriff!

COOL

Jade's managed to pull off casual-glam with this sparkly three-piece.

This checked two-piece is both cool and comfy.

Understated trainers complete this laid-back look.

Jade's channelling her inner cowgirl with those country and western tassels!

The crossover neckline adds a touch of sophistication to Jade's LBD.

STEAL HER STYLE

Go for preppy, boyish, geeky and cute with added pleats and sparkles.

33

LEIGH-ANNE

Leigh-Anne totally owns sassy streetwear!

Aviator sunglasses complete this cool-casual look.

Overlapping layers make this outfit even more eye-catching.

Leigh-Anne totally rocks this military-style jacket.

YEAH!

Leigh-Anne is a style kweeeeen in this funky neon green and black dress.

Ripped knee skinny jeans are so hot right now!

Leigh-Anne's trainers add a tiny pop of colour.

STEAL HER STYLE

Experiment with neon, leather, knee-high boots, wide belts and oversized tees.

Is it a hoody? Is it a dress? Who cares – it looks awesome whatever!

PERRIE

Boho-chic meets vintage glam in Perrie's diverse wardrobe!

LITTLE MIX FASHION

LOVE

This black/white contrast works really well.

Olive green is Perrie's colour as this satin jacket proves.

Not many can pull off PVC but Perrie certainly can!

Perrie's long belt provides a pop of colour.

Don't worry, she hasn't gone out in her PJs!

The coordinating trainers tie the look together.

Perrie nails casual chic with checked trousers and a logo tee.

STEAL HER STYLE

Look for flares, platform shoes, lots of zips, shiny fabrics and fringing.

WHAT'S UP?

Find out what Jade and Leigh-Anne are plotting by decoding the messages below.

KEY

★ = a
◆ = e
■ = t
♥ = c

W★nn★ go ou■ ■oni■◆?

★lways! Wh◆r◆ ya ■hinking?

■h◆r◆'s ★ ■op s◆♥r◆■ ♥◆l◆b
por■y w◆ ♥ould ♥r★sh.

W◆'r◆ not on
■h◆ gu◆s■ lis■?

No■ ■his ■im◆.

So how do w◆ g◆■ in?

I'v◆ go■ ★ pl★n!

Sounds in■riguing!

M◆◆■ m◆ ★■ midnigh■
★nd I'll ■◆ll ★ll…

I'm in! Ov◆r ★nd ou■!

ANSWERS ON PAGES 76-77.

LITTLE MIX-UP!

Jesy's bought some sweets to share with the girls but she's lost them inside her packed handbag! Can you help her find them amongst this muddle of stuff?

ANSWERS ON PAGES 76-77.

37

HOW TO BE A LM POPSTAR

Wanna live like a Little Mixer?
Then learn from the pros!

DREAM BIG

hAVE CONFIDENCE

The girls have oodles of confidence but it hasn't always been that way. Perrie's battled with anxiety and Jesy's struggled with body image but they've worked through their problems and have come out the other side stronger than ever before. Now they totally own everything they do!

AWESOME

Work Hard

What with albums to record, videos to make and tours to be done, the girls are always on the go. And that's not even mentioning the charity work, filming documentaries for the Beeb or designing swimwear! There's no denying it, Little Mix work their little socks off!

Follow Your Dreams

The girls all had their fair share of knockbacks before Little Mix but they didn't give up. Even now they're fully fledged popstars they're not resting on their laurels. Leigh-Anne is following her dream to design swimwear and Perrie has collaborated with footwear brand Superga. Think big, be big!

STAY POSITIVE

Positivity is contagious and luckily the Mixers are all infected! That's not to say they don't get down occasionally, but they've learnt to focus on the good and appreciate what they have.

SUPER ST★R

Be Thankful

Little Mix know they wouldn't be where they are today without their loyal army of fans (that's you, that is!) and they never forget to say thanks. In fact, when they won their second Brit award they were straight on Twitter to say ta. In the girls' own words, "We really do have the best fans in the world!" Awwwww!

Remember your Roots

They might be super celebs who are papped every time they pop to the shops, but the famous foursome haven't forgotten where they came from. They've still got their feet firmly on the ground and haven't let fame go to their heads. Good on 'em!

SONG EMOJIS

Can you translate the emojis and icons below into Little Mix songs? Just say what you see!

1 cannonball

2 secret love song

3 black magic

4 NO MORE SAD SONGS

5 THESE FOUR WALLS

6 SHOUT OUT TO MY EX

ANSWERS ON PAGES 76-77.

ARENA DASH

Little Mix want to get to their gig at the O2 without being papped. Can you guide them through the maze avoiding the cameras on the way?

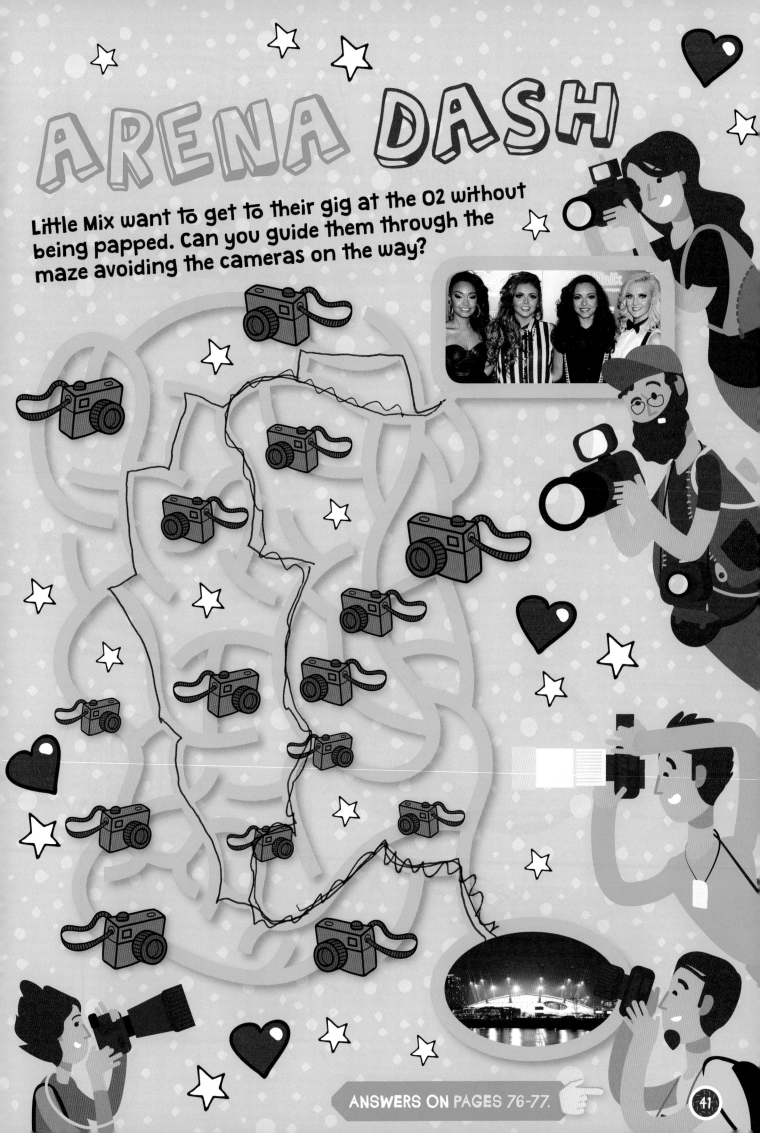

ANSWERS ON PAGES 76-77.

GET YA FACE ON!

Whether you like nice and natural or bold and dramatic, you can look to the Mixers for make-up inspo.

shine

Perrie's teamed heavy eyes with nude lips - the perf combo.

UR GR8

Jesy's red carpet ready with dramatic eyes and full lips.

Jade looks fresh-faced and natural with these neutral tones.

STAY FAB

GET THE LM LOOK

♥ Apply a subtle highlighter for glowing skin.

♥ Tame your eyebrows with with brow gel.

♥ Use liquid eyeliner for dramatic cat eyes.

♥ Dust blusher over your cheekbones for a rosy glow.

♥ Use lip liner for the perfect pout.

Leigh-Anne pulls off casual-glam with golden eyes and peach lips.

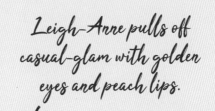

just be a QUEEN

RED CARPET READY

NAILED IT!

Grab your fave pens and design a manicure for each of the Little Mixers.

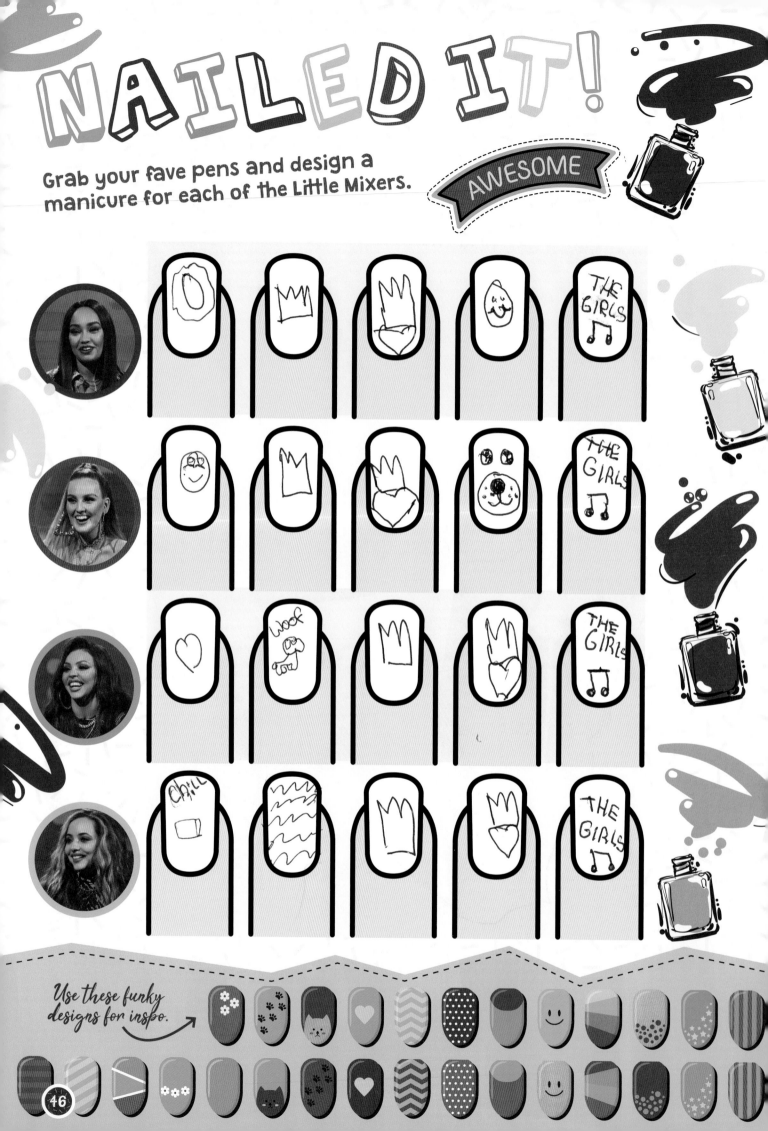

Use these funky designs for inspo.

SPOTTED!

Jesy, Jade, Leigh-Anne and Perrie are supposed to be on stage but they've snuck into the crowd! Can you find them?

The Little Mixers normally stand out from the crowd but today they're blending in!

LM INFLUENCERS

Read on to find out who's influenced Little Mix's unique sound and style. It's all about the inspo!

BRILLIANT BEYONCÉ

R&B singing sensation Beyoncé is a massive inspo for Perrie. The former Destiny's Child lead singer rose to fame in a girl group too so Perrie and Beyoncé have plenty in common!

SUPERSTAR MARIAH

Leigh-Anne grew up listening to American songstress Mariah Carey. She loved singing and dancing to Mariah's catchy tunes and performing them with her sister. Adorbs!

MARVELLOUS MISSY

Hip hop superstar Missy Elliott is one of Jesy's musical idols. She sings, she raps, she writes songs, she dances – it seems like there's nothing Missy can't do!

CHIC SISTERS

If Perrie could steal anyone's style it would be the Olsen sisters. She loves Mary Kate and Ashley's cool, chic look.

yes!

DIVA DIANA

Legendary Supremes singer Diana Ross is Jade's musical iidol. Her song, *When You Tell Me That You Love Me*, reminds Jade of her mam. Awwwwww!

STYLISH RIHANNA

Leigh-Anne loves trendsetting Rihanna's fearless fashion. When it comes to clothes, Leigh-Anne thinks Rihanna would slay in anything and everything.

With a musical mum and dad, this girl was born to sing!

GORGEOUS GWEN

Jesy looks to singer Gwen Stefani for style inspo. Gwen totally owns her bold, original outfits so it's easy to see why Jesy totes adores her look.

MUSICAL FAM

Forget world-famous divas and superstar celebs, Perrie's biggest musical inspirations are her own ma and pa! Both singers, Perrie says her parents are the most talented people she knows.

JUST FOR THE LOLs!

Even celebs don't always look perf in their pics! Add your own hilare meme captions to these Little Mix snaps.

#NoFilter

WHEN YOU REALISE 20,000 PEOPLE ARE WATCHING YOU.

Here's one to get you started.

COOL CROSSWORD

Use your skills to complete this crossword all about your fave foursome. But don't get cross if you don't know the words (geddit?)!

ACROSS

1. Little Mix's debut single (10).
2. This member was born on Boxing Day (4).
3. Perrie's middle name (6).
4. Jesy's surname (6).
5. _ _ _ _ _ _ Carey, the American singer Leigh-Anne grew up listening to (6).

DOWN

1. Little Mix's first album (3).
2. Jade and Perrie's hometown (5, 7)
3. _ _ _ _ _ *Magic*, the group's 2015 number one hit [5].
4. Missy _ _ _ _ _ _ _, American rapper featured on How Ya Doin'? (7).
5. Nicki _ _ _ _ _, who the girls collaborated with on *Woman Like Me* (5).

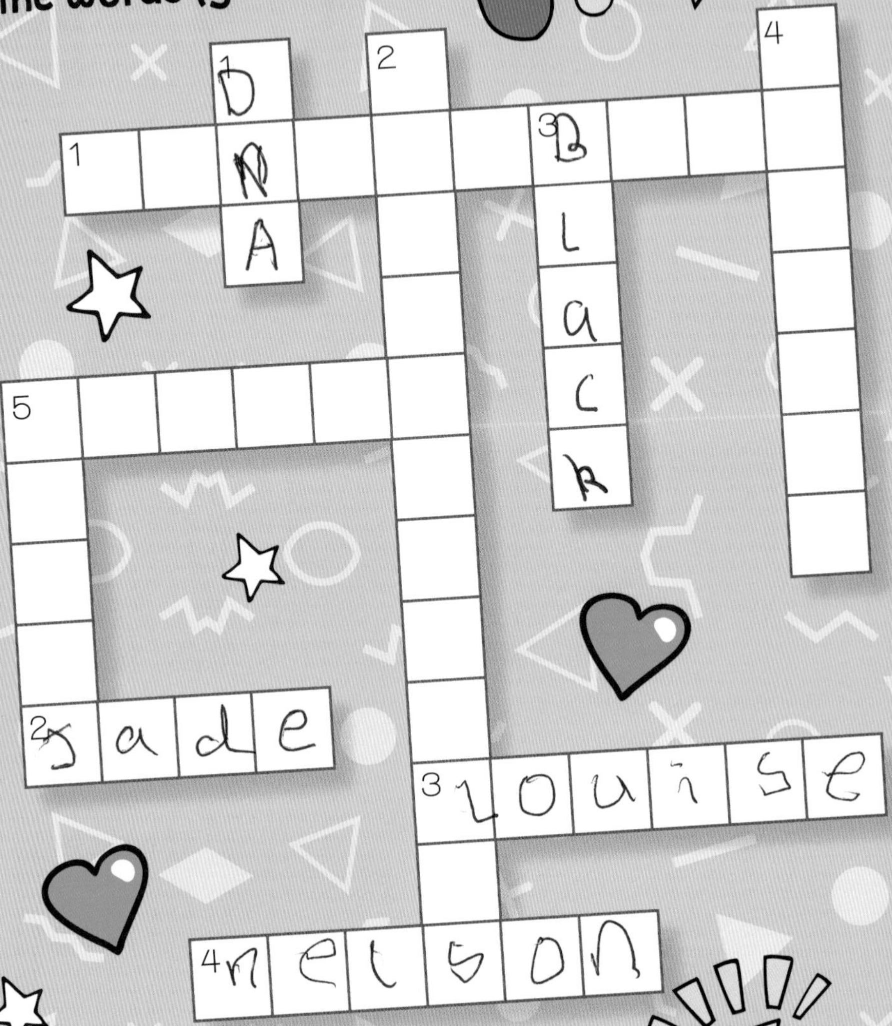

ANSWERS ON PAGES 76-77.

MYSTERY MIXER

Reads the clues below to work out which member of Little Mix is being described.

HER FAVE COLOURS ARE RED AND BLACK.

One of her musical idols is **MISSY ELLIOTT**

She loves a good curry.

She had elocution lessons to lose her regional twang.

SHE'S THE **OLDEST** IN THE BAND.

She's got loads of tattoos.

Little Mix Forever

HER MIDDLE NAME IS **LOUISE**.

She went to stage school.

THE MYSTERY MEMBER IS:

__ __ Perrie __ __ __ __

ANSWERS ON PAGES 76-77.

QUICK-FIRE FAVES!

Wanna know what rocks Little Mix's world? Here are a few of their favourite things.

JESY

FOOD:	MUSICIANS:
Curry.	Beyoncé and Missy Elliott.
COLOUR:	**ALBUM OR SONG:**
Red and black.	*Respect M.E.* by Missy Elliott, *4* by Beyoncé and *Graffiti* and *F.A.M.E.* by Chris Brown.

PERRIE

FOOD:	MUSICIANS:
Spaghetti and meatballs and mince with dumplings.	Beyoncé, Christina Aguilera and Mariah Carey.
COLOUR:	**ALBUM OR SONG:**
Blue.	Britney Spears Greatest Hits and Journey's Greatest Hits.

JADE ☆

FOOD:
Sunday roast
and lasagne.

COLOUR:
Teal, purple
and gold.

MUSICIANS:
Beyoncé and
Amy Winehouse.

LOVE

ALBUM OR SONG:
Back to Black by
Amy Winehouse,
Sigh No More by
Mumford & Sons and
Redemption Song by
Beyoncé and Eddie Vedder.

LEIGH-ANNE ☆

FOOD:
Nachos with
all the trimmings.

COLOUR:
Green.

MUSICIANS:
Rihanna, Beyoncé, Ciara,
Chris Brown and Tinashe.

ALBUM OR SONG:
Who You Are by Jessie J,
Music Box by Mariah Carey
and *U Got It Bad* by Usher.

CROWNING GLORY

The Little Mixers use their hair as the ultimate accessory! Read on for some hairstyle inspo.

We're twinsies!

Leigh-Anne's funky pineapple up-do is all sorts of amazing!

Jesy looks slick with this super sleek bob.

These loose waves really suit Jade's long locks.

GET THE LOOK

Recreate Perrie's fab bubble ponytail by following these simple steps.

STEP 1

Brush your hair and pull it back into a ponytail. Secure with a hairband.

STEP 2

Backcomb your pony tail to give your hair some volume then add another hairband a few centimetres below the first one.

STEP 3

Keep sectioning off the hair and adding hairbands until you reach the end of your ponytail. Gently pull each section outwards to loosen the hair and create the bubbles, then you're ready to swish!

BESTIE BADGES

Little Mix are BFFS who are always there for each other. Let your besties know what they mean to you with these cute LM inspired badges.

STAY FAB

GAL PAL

shine

DREAM BIG

SUPER STAR

it's gonna be okay

LIFE IS BETTER WITH YOU IN IT

UR GR8

CHIC

58

BE HAPPY

Super Star

YOU ARE AWESOME!

be BRAVE

just be a QUEEN

SELF LOVE

STAY STRONG

I'VE GOT YOUR BACK

GOOD VIBES ONLY!

YOU go GIRL

think positive

GIRL GANG

HAPPY

Make sure you read pages 57 and 60 before you cut your badges out, or photocopy these pages instead.

59

CHEEKY CHANGES

How quickly can you spot the 10 differences between these two Little Mix pix? Rate your skills opposite.

HOW'D YA DO?

Less than 2 minutes?
Ouch, you're on fire!

More than 4 minutes?
Did you fall asleep?!

2 to 4 minutes?
Could do better!

ANSWERS ON PAGES 76-77.

LM MAKEOVER

Create your own Little Mix lewk by choosing your fave items from the choice below. #slay

TOPS

BOTTOM

SHOES

Which item would Jesy totally rock?

Don't forget to accessorise!

ACCESSORIES

BFFs

GET PUZZLIN'

Train your brain with these tricky teasers!

Fill in the Blanks

Add the missing words to complete these Little Mix song titles.

1 B l a c k Magic

2 _ _ _ _ _ _ Me

3 Woman Like M e

4 _ _ _ _ _ _ About Us

5 Good _ _ _ _ _ _ _

6 _ _ _ _ _ _ Out to My _ _

7 Change Your l i f e

8 s e c r e t Love Song

9 No More s a d Songs

10 L o v e Me Or L e a v e Me

Smash Alert!

Oops, butter-fingers Leigh-Anne has dropped her phone! Can you piece her wallpaper image back together?

Whose Shoes?

Can you match the funky footwear to the correct Little Mixer?

ANSWERS ON PAGES 76-77.

POPSTAR SELFIES

Always wanted to be part of LM? Well here's your chance!
Use these props to take hilare selfies to share with your friends.

Cut out your selfie props, attach paper straws with sticky tape to hold them up, then strike a pose!

Make sure you read pages 67 and 70 before you cut out the props.

CELEB BLOG

Your wish has come true and you've become a Mixer for the day! Fill in this blog to record what you get up to.

12PM

Time to grab a bite to eat. I head to The Ivy to catch up with my celeb bestie Dani Dyer.

Here's an example for inspo.

my true LOVE

Packed Schedule

Here are some ideas of things you could include:

- ♥ Attend a press conference.
- ♥ Do a photoshoot.
- ♥ Go shopping with a celeb friend.
- ♥ Record a single.
- ♥ Pose for selfies with fans.
- ♥ Give a magazine interview.
- ♥ Go to a premiere.
- ♥ Rehearse in a studio.
- ♥ Appear on a chat show.
- ♥ Sign some autographs.
- ♥ Workout at the gym.

Don't forget to update your socials!

IT'S QUIZ TIME!

Test your Little Mix knowledge by sorting the fact from the fiction.

Question 1

Perrie's nickname is Periwinkle.
True ☑ False ☐

Question 2

Jesy went to stage school.
True ☑ False ☑

Question 3

Leigh-Anne is from South Shields.
True ☑ False ☑

Question 4

Jade used to think her mum was Diana Ross.
True ☐ False ☑

Question 5

LM won Best Group at the 2019 Brit Awards.
True ☑ False ☑

Question 6

Leigh-Anne has launched her own brand of cosmetics.
True ☑ False ☑

Question 7

Nicki Minaj features on Little Mix's *Woman Like Me.*
True ☑ False ☑

Question 8

Perrie's fave colour is blue.
True ☑ False ☑

Question 9

The other Little Mixers call Jade Poopey.
True ☑ False ☑

Question 10

Jesy and Perrie climbed Kilimanjaro for Comic Relief.
True ☐ False ☑

How did you do?

1-3 CORRECT
Sure you're a fan?!

4-7 CORRECT
Pretty good goin'!

8-10 CORRECT
Top of the class!

POP PREDICTIONS

Take a peek into the future with these Little Mix predictions. How much would you LOL if they all came true?

THE JESY SHOW

Following on from her successful documentary, Jesy gets her own chat show!

Little Mix collaborate with the Spice Girls to record the ultimate girl power anthem!

Perrie hears the patter of tiny dancing feet when she gives birth to a mini-Mixer!

All four girls become judges on The X Factor! Move over Simon Cowell!

HOLLYWOOD

The girls conquer Hollywood, starring in a movie about their rise to fame!

Leigh-Anne's swimwear range is so successful she opens a chain of high street stores!

In recognition of her loyalty, Jesy gets a Nandos burger named after her!

Not to be outdone by Jade and Leigh-Anne, Jesy and Perrie trek to Everest Base Camp!

ANSWERS

Pages 10–11

#SelfieFail
Perrie.

Spot It
B.

Jade in the Shade!
C.

Award Dash
C.

Page 20

Supersize Search

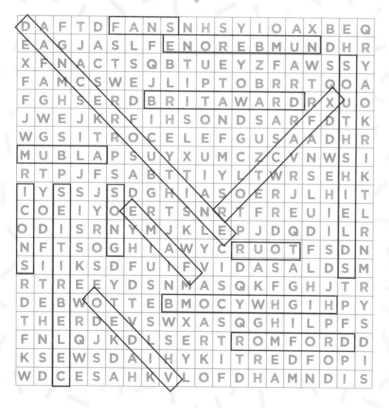

Page 21

#Be Your Selfie
a – Jade, b – Leigh-Anne,
c – Jesy, d – Perrie.

Page 36

What's Up?!

Wanna go out tonite?

Always! Where ya thinking?

There's a top secret celeb party we could crash.

We're not on the guest list?

Not this time.

So how do we get in?

I've got a plan!

Sounds intriguing!

Meet me at midnight and I'll tell all…

I'm in! Over and out!

Page 37

Little Mix-up!

Page 40

Song Emojis

1. Cannonball.
2. Secret Love Song.
3. Black Magic.
4. No More Sad Songs.
5. These Four Walls.
6. Shout Out To My Ex.

Page 41
Arena Dash

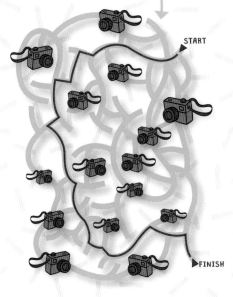

Page 47

Page 52
Cool Crossword

Page 53
Mystery Mixer
Jesy.

Pages 60–61
Cheeky Changes

Pages 66–67
Fill in the Blanks
1. Black Magic.
2. Little Me.
3. Woman Like Me.
4. Think About Us.
5. Good Enough.
6. Shout Out To My Ex.
7. Chance Your Life.
8. Secret Love Song.
9. No More Sad Songs.
10. Love Me Or Leave Me.

Smash Alert!
1. C.
2. B.
3. A.
4. G.
5. D.
6. I.

Whose Shoes?
1. C.
2. A.
3. D.
4. B.

Pages 72–73
It's Quiz Time!
1. True.
2. True.
3. False – she's from High Wycombe.
4. True.
5. False – they won Best Artist Video of the Year.
6. False – she's launched swimwear.
7. True.
8. True.
9. True.
10. False – it was Jade and Leigh-Anne.

PICTURE CREDITS